UNDERSTANDING THE LIMITS OF ARTIFICIAL INTELLIGENCE FOR WARFIGHTERS

VOLUME 2_ DISTRIBUTIONAL SHIFT IN CYBERSECURITY DATASETS

JOSHUA STEIER
ERIK VAN HEGEWALD
ANTHONY JACQUES
GAVIN S. HARTNETT
LANCE MENTHE

PREPARED FOR THE DEPARTMENT OF THE AIR FORCE
APPROVED FOR PUBLIC RELEASE; DISTRIBUTION IS UNLIMITED.

 PROJECT AIR FORCE

For more information on this publication, visit **www.rand.org/t/RRA1722-2**.

About RAND

RAND is a research organization that develops solutions to public policy challenges to help make communities throughout the world safer and more secure, healthier and more prosperous. RAND is nonprofit, nonpartisan, and committed to the public interest. To learn more about RAND, visit www.rand.org.

Research Integrity

Our mission to help improve policy and decisionmaking through research and analysis is enabled through our core values of quality and objectivity and our unwavering commitment to the highest level of integrity and ethical behavior. To help ensure our research and analysis are rigorous, objective, and nonpartisan, we subject our research publications to a robust and exacting quality-assurance process; avoid both the appearance and reality of financial and other conflicts of interest through staff training, project screening, and a policy of mandatory disclosure; and pursue transparency in our research engagements through our commitment to the open publication of our research findings and recommendations, disclosure of the source of funding of published research, and policies to ensure intellectual independence. For more information, visit www.rand.org/about/research-integrity.

RAND's publications do not necessarily reflect the opinions of its research clients and sponsors.

Published by the RAND Corporation, Santa Monica, Calif.
© 2024 RAND Corporation
RAND® is a registered trademark.

Library of Congress Cataloging-in-Publication Data is available for this publication.

ISBN: 978-1-9774-1279-9

Cover: Josef Cole/U.S. Cyber Command and Siarhei/Adobe Stock.

About This Report

This is the second report in a five-volume series addressing how artificial intelligence (AI) could be employed to assist warfighters in four distinct areas: cybersecurity, predictive maintenance, wargames, and mission planning. These areas were chosen to reflect the wide variety of potential uses and to highlight different kinds of limits to AI application. Each use case is presented in a separate volume, as it will be of interest to a different community.

This second volume describes how *distributional shift*—the divergence of current data from the data on which an AI system was trained—can significantly reduce the longevity of AI applications for cybersecurity. This volume is intended for a technical audience; the series as a whole is designed for those who are interested in warfighting and AI applications more generally. Volume 1 in the series provides a summary of the findings and recommendations from all use cases, and the other volumes provide detailed analysis of the individual use cases:

- Lance Menthe, Li Ang Zhang, Edward Geist, Joshua Steier, Aaron B. Frank, Eric Van Hegewald, Gary J. Briggs, Keller Scholl, Yusuf Ashpari, and Anthony Jacques, *Understanding the Limits of Artificial Intelligence for Warfighters*: Vol. 1, *Summary*, RR-A1722-1, 2024
- Li Ang Zhang, Yusuf Ashpari, and Anthony Jacques, *Understanding the Limits of Artificial Intelligence for Warfighters*: Vol. 3, *Predictive Maintenance*, RR-A1722-3, 2024
- Edward Geist, Aaron B. Frank, and Lance Menthe, *Understanding the Limits of Artificial Intelligence for Warfighters*: Vol. 4, *Wargames*, RR-A1722-4, 2024
- Keller Scholl, Gary J. Briggs, Li Ang Zhang, and John L. Salmon, *Understanding the Limits of Artificial Intelligence for Warfighters*: Vol. 5, *Mission Planning*, RR-A1722-5, 2024.

The research reported here was commissioned by Air Force Materiel Command, Strategic Plans, Programs, Requirements and Assessments (AFMC/A5/8/9) and conducted within the Force Modernization and Employment Program of RAND Project AIR FORCE as part of a fiscal year 2022 project, "Understanding the Bounds of Artificial Intelligence in Warfare Applications."

RAND Project AIR FORCE

RAND Project AIR FORCE (PAF), a division of the RAND Corporation, is the Department of the Air Force's (DAF's) federally funded research and development center for studies and analyses, supporting both the United States Air Force and the United States Space Force. PAF provides the DAF with independent analyses of policy alternatives affecting the development, employment, combat readiness, and support of current and future air, space, and cyber forces. Research is conducted in four programs: Strategy and Doctrine; Force Modernization and Employment; Resource Management; and Workforce, Development, and Health. The research reported here was prepared under contract FA7014-22-D-0001.

Additional information about PAF is available on our website:
www.rand.org/paf/

This report documents work originally shared with the DAF on September 23, 2022. The draft report, dated September 2022, was reviewed by formal peer reviewers and DAF subject-matter experts.

Acknowledgments

We thank our sponsor contact, Kathryn Sowers, and our action officers, Julia Phillips and Gregory Cazzell, for their guidance in choosing the use cases, for their thoughtfulness in scoping the research questions, and for working diligently with us to obtain the data necessary to conduct the many machine-learning experiments described in this series of reports. Thanks as well to R. Scott Erwin and Jean-Charles Ledé for graciously connecting us with many AI development efforts across the Air Force Research Laboratory and to David A. Kapp for discussing distributional shift.

We are also grateful to many current and former RAND colleagues, including Caolionn O'Connell, Sherrill Lingel, Osonde Osoba, and Chris Pernin for helping us shape the research agenda. Thanks to John Salmon for sharing his insights and Matthew Walsh for reviewing this volume. We could not have written these reports without their help; any errors that remain are ours alone.

Summary

This is the second report in a five-volume series that addresses the capabilities and limitations of artificial intelligence (AI) for warfighting applications. This volume concerns the problem of distributional shift in cybersecurity datasets. *Distributional shift* occurs when the data that an AI system encounters after it is deployed differ appreciably from the data on which it was trained and tested. Distributional shift can significantly degrade the performance of machine-learning (ML) models and thus limit their application. In the context of cybersecurity, distributional shift could be especially dangerous as the threat of cyberattacks continues to grow. AI-based cybersecurity systems that suffer significantly from distributional shift cannot successfully defend against future threats.

Issue

The occurrence of distributional shift can reduce the performance of ML systems. This issue is of particular relevance to cybersecurity datasets because the signatures of cyberattacks can shift rapidly and unpredictably in many different ways—the data environment is both high-dimensional and highly nonstationary. In seeking a solution to the detection of such a shift along with mitigation, we can create and enhance ML models so that they are more robust and effective. Therefore, detecting and mitigating the adverse effects of distributional shift is paramount to effectively defending against cyberattacks.

Approach

We chose several publicly available cybersecurity benchmark datasets, specifically those for network intrusion detection and malware classification, to investigate distributional shift. Each dataset is a state-of-the-art benchmark dataset used by researchers to study ML algorithm performance and to further research in the field. We used statistics-based methods and database segmentation to detect the shift, and we proposed mitigation methods.

Furthermore, we created a deep neural network for network intrusion detection and decision tree-based methods for malware classification. We used the open-source framework TensorFlow to create and use these tools and evaluated ML algorithm performance on new and recent data.

Key Findings

- Cybersecurity datasets suffer from distributional shift, especially in standard network intrusion detection and malware classification datasets.
- Distributional shift can be characterized in multiple ways, and the ease of detection depends on the dataset.

- Although data quality is important in training ML algorithms, the recency of the data is also significant.
- Cases in which the data must be recent to be useful limit the data available for training, which in turn bound AI performance.

Recommendations

- Dataset segmentation tests, such as those demonstrated in this report, should be performed to determine the significance of distributional shift for any AI system for cybersecurity. From these tests, a data decay rate can be estimated, which yields a rough estimate of the AI system's effective shelf life, after which it must be retrained with more recent data.
- Well-known statistical tests should be performed on the dataset as an additional measure to detect distributional shift.

Contents

Figures and Table

Figures

Table

Chapter 1

Introduction

Overview

The Department of the Air Force has become increasingly interested in the potential for artificial intelligence (AI) to revolutionize different aspects of warfighting.[1] For this project, the U.S. Air Force asked RAND Project AIR FORCE to consider broadly what AI can and *cannot* do in order to understand the limits of AI for warfighting applications. To address this request, we investigated the applicability of AI to four specific warfighting applications: *cybersecurity, predictive maintenance, wargames*, and *mission planning*. This report presents a discussion of the application of AI to cybersecurity.

Cybersecurity is the "set of processes, human behavior, and systems that help safeguard electronic resources."[2] It has become a critical part of the U.S. national defense.[3] In this report, we look at the use of AI systems to perform two common cybersecurity tasks: detecting network intrusions and identifying malware. In particular, we examine distributional shift, a phenomenon that can significantly limit AI effectiveness in these tasks.[4] *Distributional shift* occurs when the data that an AI system encounters after it is deployed differ appreciably from the data on which it was trained and tested.

In this report, we explain the importance of distributional shift, demonstrate that it can and does significantly limit AI effectiveness in detecting network intrusions and identifying malware, prescribe how to test for and quantify its effects, and suggest how those effects could be mitigated. This work is aimed primarily at larger organizations, such as headquarters facilities, that have the bandwidth and computing power to implement AI-enabled cybersecurity systems and to update their systems regularly. For warfighters at the tactical edge, where these resources are more limited and

---

[1] Updating Marvin Minksy's original 1968 definition, we follow previous RAND Corporation reports and define AI broadly as "the use of computers to carry out tasks that previously required human intelligence" (Marvin Minsky, ed., *Semantic Information Processing*, MIT Press, 1968, p. v). *Machine learning* (ML) is the related study of methods by which a computer can learn— methods by which a computer improves performance on a task by leveraging data. In this report, we are primarily concerned with deep learning, a subfield of ML.

[2] Sherali Zeadally, Erwin Adi, Zubair Baig, and Imran A. Khan, "Harnessing Artificial Intelligence Capabilities to Improve Cybersecurity," *IEEE Access*, Vol. 8, 2020, p. 23817.

[3] "The United States' strategic competitors are conducting cyber-enabled campaigns to erode U.S. military advantages, threaten our infrastructure, and reduce our economic prosperity. The Department must respond to these activities by . . . strengthening the cybersecurity and resilience of key potential targets" (U.S. Department of Defense, *Summary: 2018 Department of Defense Cyber Strategy*, 2018, p. 2).

[4] RAND researchers first identified distributional shift in cybersecurity datasets in Andrew J. Lohn, Jair Aguirre, Mark Ashby, Benjamin Boudreaux, Jonathan Fujiwara, Gavin S. Hartnett, Daniel Ish, John Speed Meyers, Caolionn O'Connell, and Li Ang Zhang, *Attacking Machine Learning in War*, RAND Corporation, RR-4386-AF, 2020, Not available to the general public, pp. 15–19.

compounded by increased latency, the problems associated with distributional shift would be exacerbated.[5]

This chapter details context, definitions, and methods. Chapter 2 presents our analysis of network intrusion detection datasets. Chapter 3 presents our analysis of malware identification datasets. Chapter 4 presents a summary of the findings and recommendations on the basis of these analyses.

Artificial Intelligence for Cybersecurity

The use of AI for cybersecurity tasks is relatively new but has grown quickly. A key requirement for AI is access to large amounts of high-quality data on which to train and test the model.[6] One of the larger public datasets for malware identification, the Endgame Malware BEnchmark for Research (EMBER), was released in 2018, and the authors noted at the time that "malware detection using machine learning has not received nearly the same attention in the open research community as other applications."[7] But by the end of 2020, the creators of EMBER's successor dataset observed that "the use of machine learning for malware detection is now relatively widespread."[8]

ML approaches to detect network intrusion—hacking attempts—have a longer history, but modern methods recently have seen similarly rapid growth. By 2022, IBM reported in its survey of senior industry executives that "93 percent [of companies] are either already using or considering implementation" of AI for cybersecurity in general and 85 percent of companies that use AI for cybersecurity use it to monitor network communications for suspicious activity.[9]

The effectiveness of AI systems for cybersecurity tasks, however, is less clear. Despite the prevalence of AI defenses, the average number of cyberattacks against companies rose 38 percent from 2020 to 2021, and the average success rate rose slightly from 11 percent to 12 percent, meaning that attackers are, if anything, growing more successful over time.[10] Another report noted that, from 2008 to 2022, "many of the core stats" of cybersecurity threats have not changed and the distribution of attacks by type remains "eerily similar," with network hacking most prominent followed by malware.[11]

---

[5] RAND researchers have looked at hardware and software solutions for AI at the tactical edge. See Lance Menthe, Li Ang Zhang, Gavin Hartnett, Sale Lilly, Kristin von Abel, Benjamin Boudreaux, Nihar Chhatiawala, Gary Briggs, Garrett Close, Jonathan Roberts, and Jared Mondschein, *AI at the Edge: Fielding an Expeditionary AI Capability for Army Intelligence*, RAND Corporation, RR-A1641-1, 2023, Not available to the general public.

[6] "[I]t is nothing new that data preparation and data quality are key for AI and data analytics. . . . This has been an issue since the early days" (Christoph Gröger, "There Is No AI Without Data," *Communications of the ACM*, Vol. 64, No. 11, November 2021, p. 98).

[7] Hyrum S. Anderson and Phil Roth, "EMBER: An Open Dataset for Training Static PE Malware Machine Learning Models," arXiv preprint, April 16, 2018, p. 1.

[8] Richard Harang and Ethan M. Rudd, "SOREL-20M: A Large Scale Benchmark Dataset for Malicious PE Detection," arXiv preprint, December 15, 2020, p. 1.

[9] IBM Institute for Business Value, *AI and Automation for Cybersecurity: How Leaders Succeed by Uniting Technology and Talent*, IBM, June 2022, pp. 2, 13.

[10] Based on a survey of 4,700 executives between March and April 2021 at corporations valued at more than $1 billion (Kelly Bissell, Jacky Fox, Ryan M. LaSalle, and Paolo Dal Cin, *State of Cybersecurity Resilience 2021: How Aligning Security and the Business Creates Cyber Resilience*, Accenture, 2021, Figure 2, p. 8).

[11] Verizon, *2022 Data Breach Investigations Report*, 2022, p. 16.

One reason for the failure of AI to reduce cyberattacks could be that, for better or worse, such programs have not been handed all responsibility for cybersecurity. People remain integral to cybersecurity defenses in almost every organization, and people make mistakes. A report on data breaches concluded that in 2022, "82% of breaches involved the human element. Whether it is the Use of stolen credentials, Phishing, Misuse, or simply an Error, people continue to play a very large role in incidents and breaches alike."[12]

Another reason, however, could be that AI success in the laboratory has failed to translate into real-world performance. As some researchers have observed,

> Many intrusion detection models have already been proposed by researchers claiming an accuracy of 98%+ with very limited false alarm below 1%. This high rate of accuracy attracted researchers and industry to invest money and effort to deliver effective products for the users. However, only few models are actually accepted by the industries to develop a real-world IDS [intrusion detection system].[13]

An important reason for this mismatch could be that the cybersecurity datasets on which these AI systems are trained are "inadequate" because they are "out of date and unreliable."[14] As we explain in the following section, one reason the recency of the dataset might be a persistent problem is the presence of distributional shift.

Distributional Shift

Distributional shift occurs when the dataset that an AI system encounters after it is deployed differs from the dataset on which it was trained and tested. This mismatch long has been recognized as a potential concern, as it can skew both performance and expectations: "In general, when the testing distribution differs from the training distribution, machine learning systems may not only exhibit poor performance, but also wrongly assume that their performance is good."[15]

There are different kinds of distributional shift.[16] For many AI applications, relevant datasets have two components—a set of features and a set of labels—and the objective of the AI system is to assign the correct labels to the given features. For example, an AI can be shown images of household pets and trained on those images until it can apply the appropriate label (e.g., dog or cat) to the features on the image with high accuracy. An example of distributional shift would be if the training set contained

---

[12] Verizon, 2022, p. 8.

[13] Ranjit Panigrahi and Samarjeet Borah, "A Detailed Analysis of CICIDS2017 Dataset for Designing Intrusion Detection Systems," *International Journal of Engineering & Technology*, Vol. 7, No. 3, January 2018, p. 479.

[14] Iman Sharafaldin, Arash Habibi Lashkari, and Ali A. Ghorbani, "Toward Generating a New Intrusion Detection Dataset and Intrusion Traffic Characterization," *Proceedings of the 4th International Conference on Information Systems Security and Privacy*, Funchal–Madeira, Portugal, January 22–24, 2018, p. 108.

[15] Dario Amodei, Chris Olah, Jacob Steinhardt, Paul Christiano, John Schulman, and Dan Mané, "Concrete Problems in AI Safety," arXiv preprint, July 25, 2016, p. 16.

[16] The nomenclature can be confusing because different academic disciplines use different terms. The most common types of distributional shift referred to in the literature are *covariate shift* and *concept drift*. There are also subtle variations depending on whether the differences are because of actual changes in the environment or sampling errors. For a review of the subject, see Jie Lu, Anjin Liu, Fan Dong, Feng Gu, João Gama, and Guangquan Zhang, "Learning Under Concept Drift: A Review," *IEEE Transactions on Knowledge and Data Engineering*, Vol. 31, No. 12, December 2019.

only images of long-haired dogs and the AI system is later vexed when it encounters a short-haired chihuahua. This is called *feature shift* because the features encountered by the field differ from those on which the AI was trained.[17]

There can also be *label shift*. This occurs when the features encountered are the same but the labels change. For example, if an expert later decides that a certain kind of network activity is malicious that was previously considered benign, that would affect how the AI performs and how that performance is judged. This label shift is more of a concern for cybersecurity than it might be for other applications because cybersecurity datasets are harder to construct:

> Unlike images, text and speech—which may be labeled relatively quickly, and in many cases by a non-expert—determining whether a binary file is malicious or benign can be a time consuming process for even the well-trained.[18]

However, label shift is comparatively easy to recognize and the mitigation strategy is straightforward, if labor-intensive: Revise the labels to restore consistency and retrain.

Distributional shift in cybersecurity applications can result from many factors, such as from the continuing evolution of the internet itself, which means that the digital signatures of all activity, including benign traffic, will naturally evolve as well. In this report, we look specifically at one pernicious kind of feature shift: a threat that changes unpredictably over time (also known as a *nonstationary environment*). Additionally, for simplicity, we do not consider artifacts of algorithmic bias, as this is beyond the scope of our report. It is well known that the landscape of threats is not static. Some cyberattacks, for example, are seasonal: "The frequency of ransomware attacks . . . tends to shift throughout the year, with May and June tending to see higher frequencies of attacks, while January tends to see lower."[19] In other cases, new threats emerge that have not been seen before: "Cyber reality . . . is a highly dynamic and complex nature; new threats appear constantly, and attacks are specifically tailored to circumvent known protection"[20]

Furthermore, hackers use AI to design their attacks and "threat actors are evolving their own tactics, techniques, and procedures—using artificial intelligence (AI) and automation to probe for weaknesses and unleash more efficient attacks."[21] In part because of this, new threats can quickly come to dominate the cyber environment. In 2021, for example, "[f]our out of the top five vulnerabilities exploited in 2021 were new vulnerabilities."[22]

The problem of feature shift goes beyond traditional concerns regarding overfitting. An AI is said to be *overfit* to its training data when it has been attuned to the particulars of its training set in unhelpful ways. The classic example is of an AI system designed to recognize tanks that instead learns

---

[17] See Sean Kulinski, Saurabh Bagchi, and David I. Inouye, "Feature Shift Detection: Localizing Which Features Have Shifted via Conditional Distribution Tests," *NeurIPS 2020: Thirty-Fourth Conference on Neural Information Processing Systems*, online conference, December 6–12, 2020.

[18] Anderson and Roth, 2018, p. 1.

[19] IBM Security, *X-Force Threat Intelligence Index 2022*, IBM, February 2022, p. 9.

[20] Nadine Wirkuttis and Hadas Klein, "Artificial Intelligence in Cybersecurity," *Cyber, Intelligence, and Security*, Vol. 1, No. 1, January 2017, p. 107.

[21] IBM Institute for Business Value, 2022, p. 2.

[22] And the changes can be very swift: "The Log4j vulnerability . . . was ranked number two for the year, despite only being disclosed in December" (IBM Security, 2022, p. 5).

to recognize the time of day because all the pictures of tanks happened to have been taken when the sun was casting shadows at a certain angle.[23] While overfitting could still occur, we are concerned here with an AI model that is properly fit to its training data but encounters real changes to the feature set in the field.

When only a few mean values of a feature set change—when, for example, an AI system attempting to predict the weather encounters higher average temperatures than it was trained on because of climate change—those shifts could be relatively easy to diagnose and mitigate. The AI model can simply be retrained on a dataset that extends to a somewhat wider variety of those features. But when a system has a large number of features that change unpredictably, mitigation becomes all but impossible.

The publicly available cybersecurity datasets that we use in this report for network intrusion detection and malware identification have approximately 80 and 2,000 features, respectively. (We describe these datasets in more detail in Chapters 2 and 3.) For the network intrusion detection task, enlarging the training space by just 10 percent along each of the 80 dimensions would increase the total volume of the training space by a factor of 2,000; for the malware identification task, enlarging the training space by 10 percent along each of the 2,000 dimensions would enlarge the total volume of the training space by a factor of 10^{82}, a number that is inconceivably large.[24]

In other words, the problem of unpredictable shifts cannot be solved by the straightforward method of training on a larger dataset that contains all potential cyberattacks. Indeed, no such dataset can conceivably exist. Although training on older data still has significant value for cybersecurity in general—after all, companies routinely fall victim to known vulnerabilities that have not yet been patched—such training provides limited additional value in combating the problem of distributional shift. This means that the amount of relevant data that is available to train an AI model is limited because a larger dataset cannot be built by including more time. These are all reasons why diagnosing distributional shift and understanding its implications are important to understanding how AI systems can—and cannot—be used to improve cybersecurity.[25]

Approach

In this report, we considered two cybersecurity tasks—network intrusion detection and malware identification—and analyzed them separately. We took a similar approach to diagnose distributional shift and estimate its effects over time. We used a large publicly available dataset for each task that reported real cybersecurity data over time. As illustrated in Figure 1.1, we then repeatedly segmented that data into different training and testing sets to test the model. (Note that Figure 1.1 shows a dataset with two features, but our datasets had far more dimensions.)

---

[23] Although this story is likely, it is probably AI folklore because all mentions of it are conveniently unsourced. See the extensive discussion by Gwern Branwen, "The Neural Net Tank Urban Legend," *Gwern.net* blog, July 4, 2023.

[24] Raising 1.1 to the 80th power yields approximately 2,000. Raising 1.1 to the 2,000th power is about 10^{82}.

[25] Distributional shift is not the only concern for cybersecurity datasets. Developer biases, conscious or unconscious, can also affect the value of these datasets and the AI models that are trained on them. Although these AI models can be quite powerful, they are best when deployed as part of a larger cybersecurity system that involves other methods.

Figure 1.1. Dataset Segmentation Illustration

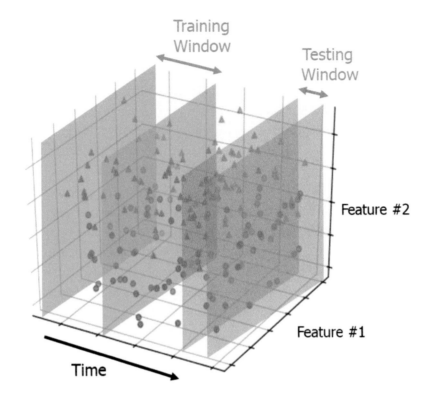

We analyzed the different sets to show that the distribution shifted over time. We then built—and rebuilt repeatedly—the same AI model with the same neural network to see how it performed on different datasets. By keeping the AI architecture the same but varying the training data, we were able to see whether the same AI system trained on earlier data worked as well on later data. This approach allowed us to rule out changes in hyperparameters or other tuning as the cause of performance degradation. It also allowed us to quantify the degradation and give an approximate timescale.

In Chapters 2 and 3, we discuss the two cases separately. In Chapter 4, we describe the major findings and recommendations.

Chapter 2

Network Intrusion Detection

A network *intrusion* is "a security event, or a combination of multiple security events, that constitutes a security incident in which an intruder gains, or attempts to gain, access to a system or system resource without having authorization to do so."[26] The nature of cybercrime continues to evolve at a rapid pace, and new generations of attacks have become more ambitious, increasing the priority for detecting zero-day attacks.[27] As the sophistication of malware and network intrusion increases, so do the methods to counter them.

There are currently two main categories of IDS: signature-based and anomaly based. A signature-based IDS uses a model of threat behavior that is based on currently known attacks. If a network traffic event matches the signature of a known attack, alarms are triggered. Since signature-based methods rely heavily on a database of known attacks, they are expected to be largely ineffective against zero-day attacks.[28] If the current trend toward more novel attacks increases, a signature-based IDS will become progressively less effective.

An anomaly based IDS instead uses a model of normal behavior and flags anything that deviates sufficiently from acceptable parameters. There are some benefits to this approach in that potential zero-day attacks might be detectable, as they should differ from normal behavior in some respect. The unpredictable nature of network intrusion and the difficulty of manually monitoring network traffic suggest that an anomaly based IDS might be superior. However, because normal behavior continues to evolve as the internet grows and changes, what appears anomalous on the basis of older models could simply be the new normal. As we will show, both signature-based and anomaly based architectures perform poorly when presented with new attacks—at least for the neural networks that we created.

---

[26] Computer Security Resource Center, Glossary, "intrusion," webpage, National Institute of Standards and Technology, undated.

[27] Ansam Khraisat, Iqbal Gondal, Peter Vamplew, and Joarder Kamruzzaman, "Survey of Intrusion Detection Systems: Techniques, Datasets and Challenges," *Cybersecurity*, Vol. 2, No. 20, 2019.

[28] A *zero-day attack* exploits a vulnerability of which even the software developer is unaware (until the attack reveals it). This differs from attacks that exploit known security issues and those that exploit the human element (such as ransomware) (Kim Zetter, "Hacker Lexicon: What Is Zero Day?" *Wired Magazine*, November 11, 2014).

Data and Methods

Datasets

For training and testing, we used two datasets released by the Canadian Institute for Cybersecurity: CIC-IDS2017 and CSE-CIC-IDS2018.[29] We chose these datasets because they are large, publicly available benchmark datasets that report network traffic and include both a wide variety of cyberattacks and unambiguously benign activity. Such datasets are typically used to develop cybersecurity applications in the commercial sector. Although a dataset consisting specifically of attacks against U.S. government systems might look different, the same issues of distributional shift would be expected for the same reasons: adaptive adversaries and the general evolution of internet behaviors. Therefore, we use these datasets as good proxies to study distributional shift. The implications are the same regardless of the exact dataset used.

The CIC-IDS2017 dataset contains the most up-to-date attacks as of 2017. The Canadian Institute for Cybersecurity used 25 simulated users to simulate network traffic for a local network over one week. Monday is a normal day that has only benign traffic. The rest of the days exhibit cyberattacks of various kinds, including brute force file transfer protocol (FTP), brute force secure socket shell (SSH), denial of service, distributed denial of service, Heartbleed, web attack, infiltration, and Botnet. The dataset includes the raw network traffic—full packet payloads in packet capture (.pcap) format—and comma-separated value (.csv) files with extracted features. The full dataset is 450 gigabytes and includes about 20 million network traffic events.

The CSE-CIC-IDS2018 dataset is of a similar size and was generated in a similar manner but with the intent to add a more dynamic component for researchers.[30] The additional component is an attacking infrastructure that includes 50 machines and a victim organization of five departments made up of 420 machines and 30 servers. As with the CIC-IDS2017 dataset, the 2018 dataset includes the captured network traffic and system logs of each machine.[31] Although there could be some mismatch between the two datasets because the ways in which the cyberattacks and benign events were generated are different, their designs enable them to be used together. The datasets are also similar in the following ways:

- First, the overwhelming majority of benign activity in both cases involves hypertext transfer protocol (HTTP) and hypertext transfer protocol secure (HTTPS). This means that the network statistics captured by the flow meter are very similar even though the number of users and connections differs.
- Second, the majority of cyberattacks in 2017 is similar in 2018. There are a few label offsets, but approximately 13 of the 15 labels are distinctly similar. The other labels could be dropped or placed together into an "other" category to synchronize the datasets.

---

[29] Sharafaldin, Lashkari, and Ghorbani, 2018.

[30] Canadian Institute for Cybersecurity, "CSE-CIC-IDS2018 on AWS," University of New Brunswick, webpage, undated.

[31] Each dataset has 80 features extracted from the captured traffic using CICFlowMeter-V3.

Neural Networks

To evaluate the effect of distributional shift over time on AI system performance, we designed, trained, and tested two neural network architectures to perform both signature detection and anomaly detection. At the high level, a *neural network* is a biologically inspired tool designed to learn from data. A neural network contains nodes that are analogous to neurons and edges that are analogous to synapses. The nodes follow a set of mathematical rules that allow flow through the network by activating certain nodes and not others. Much like how the brain makes decisions, the neural network can be used to make predictions and decisions. We used the open-source framework TensorFlow to create and use these tools.[32] While other AI methods could have been used (such as k-nearest neighbors or random forest), neural networks and the deep learning they allow continue to drive interest in AI broadly. Figure 2.1 depicts the two neural network architectures that we created.

Figure 2.1. Artificial Intelligence Architectures Used for Intrusion Detection System Case

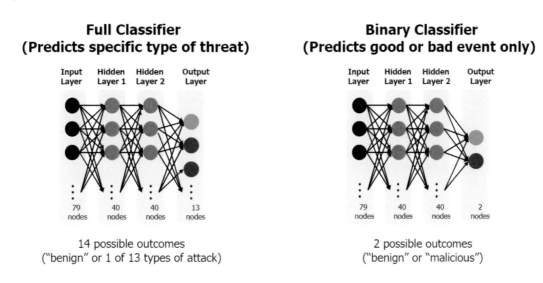

The two architectures are identical except for the final layer, which allows the full classifier 14 different outputs (one benign label and 13 different malicious attacks), while the binary classifier marks an event as either benign or malicious without trying to determine the nature of the attack. The binary classifier might be sufficient from a purely defensive standpoint, but understanding the full nature of the threat is also of value.

The novel aspect of our research approach is that, rather than tuning the hyperparameters (such as the number of layers or the number of neurons per layer) of each of these models to boost performance, we kept all architectural parameters fixed at their initial levels and varied only the data

---

[32] Martín Abadi, Ashish Agarwal, Paul Barham, Eugene Brevdo, Zhifeng Chen, Craig Citro, Greg S. Corrado, Andy Davis, Jeffrey Dean, Matthieu Devin, Sanjay Ghemawat, Ian Goodfellow, Andrew Harp, Geoffrey Irving, Michael Isard, Rafal Jozefowicz, Yangqing Jia, Lukasz Kaiser, Manjunath Kudlur, Josh Levenberg, Dan Mané, Mike Schuster, Rajat Monga, Sherry Moore, Derek Murray, Chris Olah, Jonathon Shlens, Benoit Steiner, Ilya Sutskever, Kunal Talwar, Paul Tucker, Vincent Vanhoucke, Vijay Vasudevan, Fernanda Viégas, Oriol Vinyals, Pete Warden, Martin Wattenberg, Martin Wicke, Yuan Yu, and Xiaoqiang Zheng, *TensorFlow: Large-Scale Machine Learning on Heterogeneous Systems*, preliminary white paper, Google Research, November 9, 2015.

used to train and test the models. This approach enabled us to isolate the effects of different time-phased datasets on AI system performance.

To obtain the initial architectural parameters and ensure that we had properly functioning neural networks, we first trained and tested the base models across the entire dataset using an 80/20 training-to-testing ratio—a typical split for neural net construction.[33] The results are shown in Figure 2.2.

Figure 2.2. Artificial Intelligence Accuracy Across Training

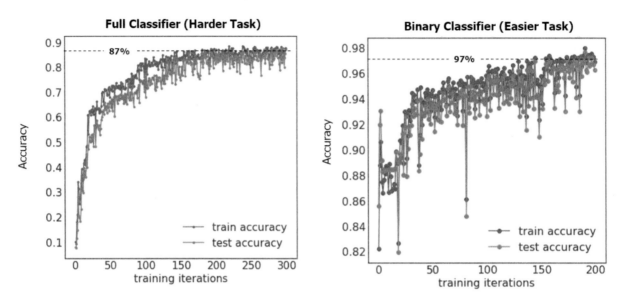

NOTE: The scales on the two graphs are not the same. *Accuracy* refers to the number of network events correctly classified divided by the total number of network events.

Figure 2.2 confirms that both classifiers provide reasonably high performance when applied to the full dataset. (Note that the scales of the graphs differ to show internal structure; despite appearances, the binary classifier is more accurate and exhibits less variance than the full classifier.) When run against randomized samples of the full dataset, the binary classifier was able to reliably distinguish benign network traffic from cyberattacks about 97 percent of the time; the full classifier was able to reliably distinguish benign network traffic from cyberattacks and also determine the nature of the cyberattack with about 87-percent accuracy. (The lower level of accuracy by the full classifier was because of the additional complexity of the task. If the full classifier correctly characterized a network traffic event as a cyberattack but wrongly identified the type of attack, this was counted as a failure. This is one reason why we created the binary classifier for comparison.)[34]

---

[33] "Empirical studies show that the best results are obtained if we use 20-30% of the data for testing, and the remaining 70-80% of the data for training" (Afshin Gholamy, Vladik Kreinovich, and Olga Kosheleva, "Why 70/30 or 80/20 Relation Between Training and Testing Sets: A Pedagogical Explanation," Departmental Technical Reports [Computer Science], University of Texas at El Paso, February 2018, p. 1).

[34] Nearly all the confusion came from misclassifying one type of an attack as another rather than misclassifying an attack as benign traffic.

Having achieved these performance levels against the full dataset, we then froze the architectures and proceeded to segment the data to investigate AI performance over time. We did this in two ways: first, by looking within the initial 2017 dataset and then by comparing the 2017 and 2018 datasets. We discuss the segmentation schemes and their results in the next section.

Results

Day-over-Day

We first searched within the original 2017 dataset for the possible effects of distributional shift over time. This dataset covers eight consecutive days of network traffic. We segmented the data by day and trained and tested on those segments to simulate an operational scenario.

In this simulated scenario, a cybersecurity operator is asked to construct an AI system to detect cyberattacks on their organization. The operator sets up a data collection mechanism and has access to new data one day at a time. The question for the operator is, When is the model good enough that it can be relied on to successfully direct systems to prevent attacks? The segmentation of training and testing data could be thought of as historical data and new data, respectively. So, for example, on day 6, the model was trained on six days of historical network data and then evaluated on the following two days of network traffic events. The value of this approach is that it simulates tactically what an actual cybersecurity operator might experience. Figure 2.3 shows the data segmentation scheme.

Figure 2.3. Data Segmentation Scheme

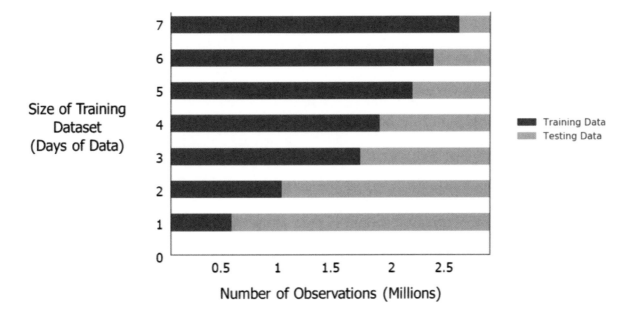

Given that most neural networks are expected to do better when trained on more data, as shown in Figure 2.2, the naive expectation would be that the performance of the AI system should improve with each additional day that the operator waits to collect data before deploying the system. Figure 2.4 shows, however, that the result is just the opposite.

Figure 2.4. Day-over-Day Segmentation Results

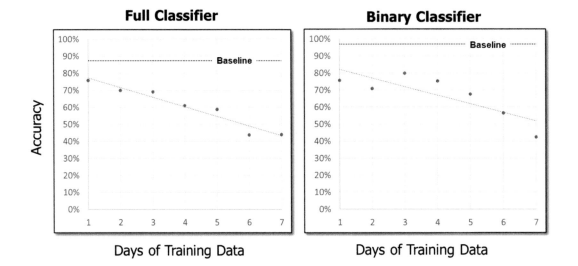

NOTE: The baseline is a random sample split of 80/20 between training and testing data of the full sample, just as in the initial setup.

Each model shows a day-over-day decline in performance by about 4 to 5 percentage points. One reason for this surprising degradation is the stark shift in the distribution of cyberattacks over the eight days. The first day contains only benign data while subsequent days contain an increasing number and variety of cyberattacks. Critically, neither AI system is able to recognize previously unseen types of cyberattacks when they first appear, and such attacks constitute an increasingly large share of the remaining dataset. As a result, training the AI system on extra days of early data does not help it classify network traffic more accurately; rather, it mistrains the AI model on irrelevant data, overfitting it to a dataset that proves increasingly obsolete. Moreover, a closer inspection of the earliest-deployed AI system reveals that it is not as successful as it might have appeared to be. The AI systems trained only on the first day both achieve 78-percent accuracy simply by labeling all network traffic as benign.

The message is clear: AI systems for cybersecurity might appear to perform well when they can sample the entire dataset over time, but this performance can be deceptive. In the real world, new attacks and tactics arise regularly, and yesterday's benchmark might be far from tomorrow's performance.

Year-over-Year

The 2017 dataset was, as noted previously, somewhat artificially constructed. It is possible that the pattern of cyberattacks encountered in the field would be less pronounced in terms of the distributional shift. To test this, we compared the 2017 dataset with the 2018 dataset. Specifically, we segmented the network traffic data to use the full 2017 dataset for training and the full 2018 dataset for testing. The 2018 dataset contained three new attacks, so we restructured the neural network to allow for this in both cases. The results are shown in Figure 2.5.

Figure 2.5. Year-over-Year Performance

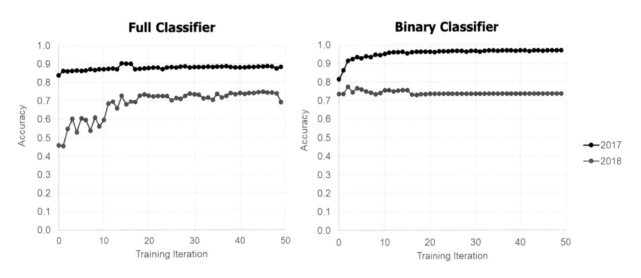

Figure 2.5 shows that an AI system trained on the 2017 data performs significantly worse on the 2018 data. Consistent with the results established earlier, the full classifier, which achieved 87- to 88-percent accuracy on the 2017 data, achieves only 73-percent accuracy on the 2018 dataset—a performance degradation of about 15 percentage points in a year. Likewise, the accuracy of the binary classifier drops from the previous value of about 97 percent to the same level as the full classifier, or about 25 percentage points, in a year. This is a slower decline than we saw within each dataset but confirms the main finding: AI is not able to adequately account for distributional shift, which poses significant problems for cybersecurity.

Because the new year contains new types of attacks, we expected reduced performance—but the problems run deeper. Even though the models are performing inference on data of the same format, same structure, and similar origin (i.e., computer network traffic as opposed to cellular network traffic or some other form of network traffic), their performance is degraded even when classifying the *same types* of attacks in the 2018 dataset that were present in the 2017 dataset because both the attacks and the benign events are subtly different.

Chapter 3

Malware Detection

Malware detection is crucial to many information systems, as malicious software can have catastrophic consequences. With the rise in the use of ransomware, the impetus for advancing malware detection methods is clear. The attack on the energy company Colonial Pipeline, for instance, consisted of ransomware that led to a halt in pipeline operations and resulted in disastrous consequences for both the company and the oil infrastructure base writ large.[35] There has been a shift toward using ML methods that can efficiently detect and classify malware. Such systems have the potential to assist in the prevention of malware-based cyberattacks. To further research in this field, many researchers have sought to establish standard datasets that could be used to benchmark ML models. Much in the spirit of the Modified National Institute of Standards and Technology (MNIST) dataset, researchers have proposed EMBER, Sophos-Reversing Labs–20 Million (SOREL-20M), and other databases as benchmarks for malware classification.[36]

Classification is a type of ML problem in which discrete labels are assigned to data using an ML algorithm. In its simplest form, the classification is binary: either malicious or benign. At the more granular level, a classification problem can be defined as how the malicious category is broken down into distinct types of malware. Most state-of-the-art methods use this more complicated classification scheme, which can be applied either as a multiclass or multilabel classification. Multiclass classification is an extension of the binary classification problem using three or more classes. Multilabel classification applies multiple labels to the same data.

Data and Methods

The essential task is the static detection of malicious Microsoft Windows portable executable files.[37] All the datasets that we used for malware classification are proposed benchmark datasets.

The EMBER dataset consists of features extracted from 1.1 million binary files; 900,000 training samples; and 200,000 test samples. More specifically, the EMBER dataset consists of JavaScript Object Notation (JSON) objects that contain different types of data. These data include the Secure

---

[35] The malware did not directly shut down pipeline operations: Colonial Pipeline chose to cease pipeline operations in response to the discovery of malware in its office systems from fear that the pipeline operations software also might be compromised—and from concern that the company might not be able to bill for the fuel (David E. Sanger and Nicole Perlroth, "Pipeline Attack Yields Urgent Lessons About U.S. Cybersecurity," *New York Times*, May 14, 2021).

[36] For the MNIST database, see Yann LeCun, Corinna Cortes, and Christopher J. C. Burges, "The MNIST Database of Handwritten Digits," undated; for the paper that introduced it, see Yann LeCun, Léon Bottou, Yoshua Bengio, and Patrick Haffner, "Gradient-Based Learning Applied to Document Recognition," *Proceedings of the IEEE*, Vol. 86, No. 11, November 1998; Anderson and Roth, 2018; and Harang and Rudd, 2020.

[37] *Static detection* (as opposed to dynamic detection) is analysis performed without actually running the software.

Hash Algorithm–256 (sha256) hash of the original file, an estimation of when the file was first seen, a binary classification label, and eight groups of features.[38] The 900,000 training samples are split evenly into 300,000 malicious samples; 300,000 benign; and 300,000 unlabeled. The groups of features together represent 2,000 different parameters for each file. EMBER consists of roughly 3.2 gigabytes of binary files collected from 2017 and 2018. The collection timeline will be discussed as a limitation in the ML models employed to perform malware classification.

The standard ML technique used with this dataset is the gradient-boosted decision tree (GBDT). This is essentially an ensemble technique applied to decision trees, whereby weak decision trees are combined to perform better. Decision trees are useful for AI interpretability and scalability, but GBDTs turn this strength on its head—instead of a small number of branches, the ensemble of weak decision trees could include hundreds of branches. Therefore, the state-of-the-art methods consist of GBDTs, such as LightGBM and XGBoost, which offer better interpretability and scalability than other GBDTs.[39] LightGBM in particular was employed by the authors that proposed EMBER.

The second dataset used in this study is SOREL-20M.[40] This is an especially large dataset (8 terabytes) with 20 million executables (hence the name SOREL-20M). The increase in data is intended to further assist in malware classification benchmark datasets, as more data can help build higher-quality ML models. We will soon see, however, that simply increasing the amount of data is not a sufficient method to create high-quality ML models.

SOREL-20M consists of extracted features plus real (but disarmed) malware samples. The samples are identified by their sha256 hash, and this is the case even for disarmed samples. The data consists of more recent data than EMBER, collected from January 2017 to early April 2019. The training set is from 2017 and 2018, whereas the test set is from 2019 data. The samples consist of tags, such as "adware," "ransomware," and "spyware" to indicate the type of malicious behavior. The authors use a LightGBM framework for malware classification along with a deep neural network—a neural network with many hidden layers. This dataset has the advantage over EMBER in terms of number of samples and more recent data.

The third dataset used is from Blue Hexagon Open Dataset for Malware Analysis (BODMAS), which consists of EMBER, SOREL-20M, and newer and better labeled data.[41] For instance, some of the samples are from 2020, whereas the SOREL-20M dataset stops in 2019 and EMBER in 2018.

---

[38] sha256 is one of many well-known cryptographic hash functions: algorithms that generate arrays of fixed size from arbitrary data. (As the name implies, this hash produces a 256-bit array as output.) Hash functions are useful because they generate short, unique signatures for data files that are mathematically almost impossible to spoof; it is essentially impossible to design two different data files that have the same hash. In this case, 0 = benign and 1 = malicious. (There is technically a third label, −1, which means that no classification has been applied.)

[39] Guolin Ke, Qi Meng, Thomas Finley, Taifeng Wang, Wei Chen, Weidong Ma, Qiwei Ye, and Tie-Yan Liu, "LightGBM: A Highly Efficient Gradient Boosting Decision Tree," *NIPS'17: Proceedings of 31st Conference on Neural Information Processing Systems*, Curran Associates, December 2017; Tianqi Chen and Carlos Guestrin, "XGBoost: A Scalable Tree Boosting System," *Proceedings of the 22nd ACM Special Interest Group on Knowledge Discovery and Data Mining (SIGKDD) International Conference on Knowledge Discovery and Data Mining*, San Francisco, California, August 13–17, 2016.

[40] Harang and Rudd, 2020.

[41] Limin Yang, Arridhana Ciptadi, Ihar Laziuk, Ali Ahmadzadeh, and Gang Wang, "BODMAS: An Open Dataset for Learning Based Temporal Analysis of PE Malware," *2021 IEEE Symposium on Security and Privacy Workshops*, San Francisco, California, May 27, 2021.

BODMAS was mainly used as an improvement to both EMBER and SOREL-20M to understand the importance of more recent data.

In this work, we sought to examine and mitigate distributional shift in ML models trained on these benchmark datasets. We used LightGBM as our AI method and used statistical techniques, such as the Kolmogorov-Smirnov (KS) test, to quantify how much a distribution shifts over time.[42]

Results

The first step in understanding distributional shift in an ML model is to be able to confirm the underlying distributional shift. We employ the KS test to determine if distributional shift is present.[43] The KS test is a statistical method used to test how likely it is that a given sample was derived from a given probability distribution. It can be used in a straightforward manner to compare whether two probability distributions are the same. The output of the test is a p-value for the null hypothesis: The closer the value is to zero, the more likely that the distributions are not the same.[44]

To test for distributional shift over time, we split the SOREL-20M dataset into two halves—2017 and 2018—and tested whether the data from 2018 are from the same distribution as the data from 2017. (It should be noted that the datasets here are much larger than those used for detecting network intrusion and with far more parameters—for this reason, we had to confine ourselves to a simpler data segmentation scheme for this analysis.) The results are given in Table 3.1.

---

[42] The KS test is commonly used to determine whether a sample comes from a given distribution. It is implemented in most major software packages. See Ana Justel, Daniel Peña, and Rubén Zamar, "A Multivariate Kolmogorov-Smirnov Test of Goodness of Fit," *Statistics & Probability Letters*, Vol. 35, No. 3, 1997.

[43] Unfortunately, a practical issue with the IDS dataset format prevented us from employing the same KS test on that data in a reasonable time frame.

[44] Technically, we use the KS test with the Bonferroni correction. Essentially, we divide the required p-value by the dimensionality of the dataset. (Thus, for 2,000 dimensions, instead of using a p-value of 0.05, we demand a much smaller p-value of ~2.5×10^{-5}.) This correction is necessary to account for the possibility that a KS test along any given dimension might succeed by random chance. See J. Martin Bland and Douglas G. Altman, "Multiple Significance Tests: The Bonferroni Method," *BMJ*, Vol. 310, January 21, 1995, p. 170. This method has been shown to perform as accurately as other multivariate statistical tests (Justel, Peña, and Zamar, 1997).

Table 3.1. Kolmogorov-Smirnov Test Results

Tag	p-Value
Adware	1.4×10^{-13}
Flooder	8.013×10^{-11}
Ransomware	2.8×10^{-3}
Dropper	0.0
Spyware	0.0
Crypto Miner	0.0
File Infector	0.0
Installer	0.0
Worm	8.215×10^{-7}
Downloader	7.593×10^{-11}

As is evident from Table 3.1, the p-values for each type of malware are vanishingly small. It is extremely unlikely that the 2018 samples are drawn from the same distribution as the 2017 samples. In other words, malware has evolved, and we see this trend clearly in the changed distribution of the approximately 2,000 extracted features.

To examine the data further, we looked at the BODMAS dataset. BODMAS was created using the same format as EMBER and SOREL-20M to extend that data for another year or so. (The previous datasets cover 2017 and 2018, respectively; BODMAS extends coverage through 2019.) In this case, we used the earlier SOREL-20M dataset to train the AI system and then tested it on different segments of the BODMAS data. Figure 3.1 shows this data segmentation scheme.

Figure 3.1. Data Segmentation Plan

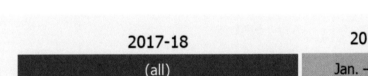
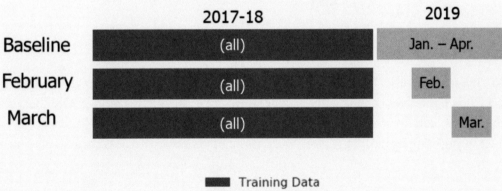

NOTE: The April data are incomplete, and the January data showed no noticeable differences.

The baseline case uses the entire BODMAS dataset to test the AI system. The February and March segments use only BODMAS data from those respective months to test. We show the results using receiver operating characteristic (ROC) curves by changing the test data. A ROC curve is a plot of the true positive rate (TPR) against the false positive rate (FPR) for an algorithm.[45] We use this particular representation so we can compare our results directly with those in the original BODMAS paper.[46] In the baseline ROC curve shown in Figure 3.2, we trained the AI system on the SOREL-20M dataset and then ran it on 2019 BODMAS.

Figure 3.2. Baseline Receiver Operating Characteristic Curves

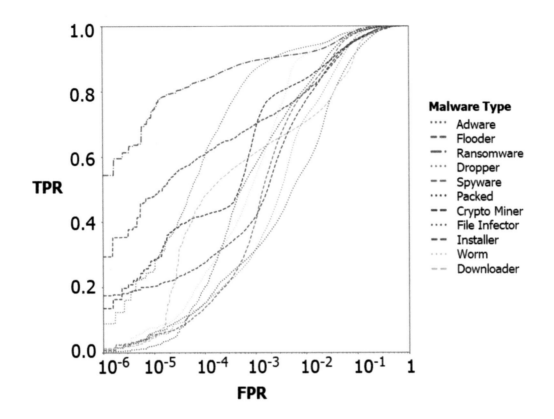

NOTE: FPR is plotted on a logarithmic scale.

The results shown in Figure 3.2 confirm what was reported in the original BODMAS paper. Note that while the TPR is plotted on the usual linear scale from 0 to 1, the FPR is plotted on a logarithmic scale so that the details of its structure can be more clearly displayed. The actual FPR is, therefore, much lower than it might appear at first glance: Most of the FPRs shown are less than 10 percent.

---

[45] The ROC curves were originally created by radar engineers in World War II. The true and false positive rates were considered key operating characteristics of the receiver.

[46] Yang et al., 2021.

Figures 3.3 and 3.4 show the ROC curves for the same AI architecture but tested only on subsets of the BODMAS data from February and March 2019, respectively.

Figure 3.3. February 2019 Receiver Operating Characteristic Curves

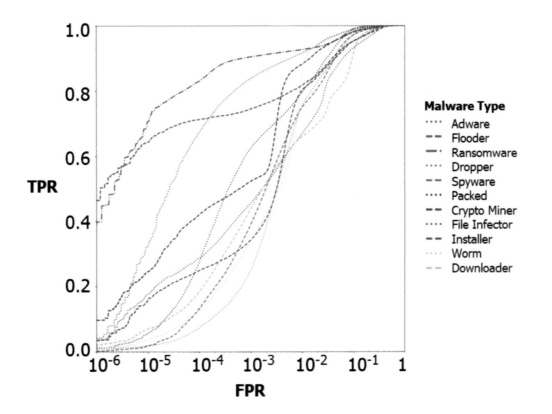

NOTE: FPR is plotted on a logarithmic scale.

Figure 3.4. March 2019 Receiver Operating Characteristic Curves

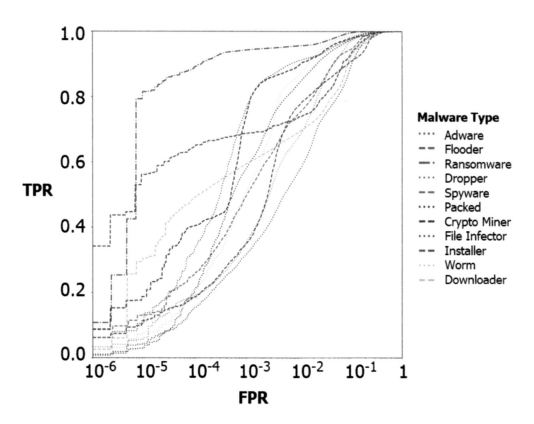

NOTE: FPR is plotted on a logarithmic scale.

Using the baseline for comparison, we can see a subtle decrease in performance over time for the tags. More specifically, the adware and flooder types of malware show the largest shift in performance, primarily in the TPR. This decrease in performance on the basis of the test set is an indicator of a subtle distributional shift. Coupled with the KS test, we determined that distributional shift exists for the ML model trained on this dataset.

Because the shifts were small, we looked for longer-term distributional shifts. Following a similar method to the ROC curves, we looked at the change in the F_1 score by keeping the training set the same but changing the test set month by month.[47] We also compared it with the original results from the 2017–2018 test. The results are shown in Figure 3.5.

---

[47] The F_1 score for classification is the harmonic mean of the precision and recall statistics. *Precision* is the ratio of the number of correctly classified objects (true positives) to the total number of objects assigned this classification (true positives plus false positives). *Recall* is the ratio of the number of correctly classified objects to the total number of objects that should have been classified this way (true positives plus false negatives). The F_1 score runs from 0 (worst) to 1 (best). The F_1 score is often used as a single statistical measure of goodness because, due to its construction, it is only high if both precision and recall are high.

Figure 3.5. Year-over-Year Segmentation Test

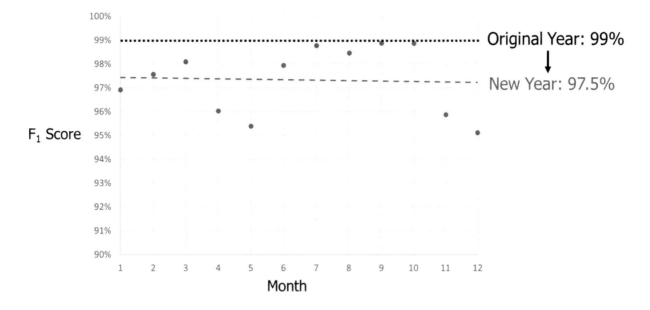

Figure 3.5 shows that when AI performance is judged on a month-to-month basis, there is some variation—the F_1 scores of the blue dots representing the month-to-month scores range from 95 percent to 99 percent—but taken as a whole, AI performance on this subsequent year of data is lower than it was with the original dataset. The degradation of performance is clear, but only by 1–2 percent.[48]

These methods show that distributional shift is both real and has an effect on malware identification, but it is smaller than the shift seen in network intrusion detection. This means that the benchmark databases for malware identification, and the AI systems trained on them, will have a longer shelf life than those for network intrusion detection. Nevertheless, the methods also illustrate that even these cybersecurity models will have an expiration date. Assuming this level of degradation persists, in a few years, the performance will fall appreciably. Furthermore, if adversaries increase their use of AI methods to adapt to network intrusion detection measures, the shelf lives of future trained AI systems could become significantly shorter.

In a world in which acquisition can be slow, it is important to be able to recognize and test for this kind of AI performance before a system is acquired so that appropriate expectations can be set. This finding also reinforces the point made earlier that these ML models benefit mainly from the recency of data rather than the raw quality or the amount of data. And because there is only a certain amount of data available in any given time frame, that places an effective limit on the success of AI.

---

[48] In Chapter 2, we used two different IDS models in which misclassification within the malicious class was counted as a failure in one and not in the other. In this case, for malware detection, we used only one model—the former—as a proof of concept. Different models that count any correct classification as malicious as a success, even if the software was misidentified, might be equally useful in practice and might display a different decay rate.

Chapter 4

Conclusion

Distributional shift is a significant factor in cybersecurity datasets. Because cybersecurity failures can result in disastrous consequences, they merit attention.

For standard network intrusion detection ML models, distributional shift causes a decline in performance that can be seen in day-over-day results and year-over-year results using the dataset segmentation approach that we applied. While the dramatic fall in day-over-day performance might be due in part to the artificial construction of the benchmark dataset, the year-over-year results are not. Those results saw the simple binary classification algorithm decline from 97-percent effectiveness to 73-percent effectiveness, which means that the algorithm is falling well out of tolerance in a matter of months. One reason for the degradation is that hackers are adaptive and create new attacks specifically designed to fool AI systems. As a result, the AI systems could not anticipate or recognize cyberattacks they had not previously seen. While it is possible that more complex AI systems than the ones we built could suffer less decline, the high-dimensional, highly dynamic nature of the cybersecurity environment precludes any hope that ML algorithms can anticipate even a fraction of new attacks.

The standard malware classification dataset-based ML models showed little month-to-month change and a much slower year-over-year shift. This is because the distributional shift in malware was more subtle than in the case of network intrusion. Whereas the AI systems observing network traffic faced significantly different kinds of cyberattacks, the AI systems observing malware faced subtle but pernicious changes. The decline was less dramatic but still clearly evident at 1.5 to 2 percent per year, and this rate of decline will compound over time.

Distributional shift does not only exist in cybersecurity benchmark datasets. This shift can also exist in other datasets, such as climate or financial datasets. It can be present in aircraft maintenance databases, which we took into account in our design of the ML models described in Volume 3 of this series.[49] It can also be present in the case of aircraft mission planning, for which *pop-up emitters* (previously unknown enemy radar systems that suddenly are turned on) can change the threat landscape in ways that can be difficult to predict in advance.[50] Therefore, the impact of degradation on the ML models has the potential to affect many different systems and to lead to potentially disastrous consequences. It is important to note that the quality of the datasets matters, but more significantly, recency matters as well. Because of this, there is a limit and bound to the ML system in which new

---

[49] Li Ang Zhang, Yusuf Ashpari, and Anthony Jacques, *Understanding the Limits of Artificial Intelligence for Warfighters: Vol. 3, Predictive Maintenance*, RAND Corporation, RR-A1722-3, 2024.

[50] Keller Scholl, Gary J. Briggs, Li Ang Zhang, and John L. Salmon, *Understanding the Limits of Artificial Intelligence for Warfighters: Vol. 5, Mission Planning*, RAND Corporation, RR-A1722-5, 2024.

data are not always available. ML systems should be periodically retrained on new data as a method of mitigation. Statistical-based methods and dataset segmenting tests can effectively detect distributional shift and, coupled with such mitigation approaches as retraining, can allow for more robust ML systems.

For this reason, we make one major recommendation: Dataset segmentation tests, such as those presented in this report, should be performed for any AI-based cybersecurity system to assess the likely significance of distributional shift on performance over time. These tests can be used to estimate a data decay rate, which in turn can be used to yield an estimate of the likely shelf life of an AI system before it must be completely retrained. When multiple datasets are available from different periods, these same tests can be used to extrapolate a shelf life, after which the automated IDS or ML detection system must be retrained.[51]

We also recommend that well-known statistical tests, such as the KS test, be performed on the dataset as an additional measure to detect or confirm distributional shift. We note that the degradation was subtle over time for the malware classification task, but the KS test was unambiguous in showing that a shift of some kind had occurred.

Distributional shift is a special problem for AI-enabled cybersecurity applications because the cyber landscape is constantly changing in unpredictable ways: Malign software and network activity shift over time because our adversaries are highly adaptive, and benign software and network activity shift over time because the internet is evolving. In this report, we have demonstrated how to detect, quantify, and mitigate the effects of distributional shift to make AI-enabled malware detection and network intrusion detection applications more robust. Future work should consider how these methods can be extended to a broader variety of cybersecurity applications and what additional methods would be required to do so at the tactical edge.

---

[51] While day-over-day or year-over-year data are sufficient to estimate a decay rate, data from three or more distinct periods would be recommended to extrapolate further.

Abbreviations

AI	artificial intelligence
BODMAS	Blue Hexagon Open Dataset for Malware Analysis
EMBER	Endgame Malware BEnchmark for Research
FPR	false positive rate
GBDT	gradient-boosted decision tree
IDS	intrusion detection system
KS	Kolmogorov-Smirnov
ML	machine learning
ROC	receiver operating characteristic
sha256	Secure Hash Algorithm–256
SOREL-20M	Sophos-Reversing Labs–20 Million
TPR	true positive rate

References

Abadi, Martín, Ashish Agarwal, Paul Barham, Eugene Brevdo, Zhifeng Chen, Craig Citro, Greg S. Corrado, Andy Davis, Jeffrey Dean, Matthieu Devin, Sanjay Ghemawat, Ian Goodfellow, Andrew Harp, Geoffrey Irving, Michael Isard, Rafal Jozefowicz, Yangqing Jia, Lukasz Kaiser, Manjunath Kudlur, Josh Levenberg, Dan Mané, Mike Schuster, Rajat Monga, Sherry Moore, Derek Murray, Chris Olah, Jonathon Shlens, Benoit Steiner, Ilya Sutskever, Kunal Talwar, Paul Tucker, Vincent Vanhoucke, Vijay Vasudevan, Fernanda Viégas, Oriol Vinyals, Pete Warden, Martin Wattenberg, Martin Wicke, Yuan Yu, and Xiaoqiang Zheng, *TensorFlow: Large-Scale Machine Learning on Heterogeneous Systems*, preliminary white paper, Google Research, November 9, 2015.

Amodei, Dario, Chris Olah, Jacob Steinhardt, Paul Christiano, John Schulman, and Dan Mané, "Concrete Problems in AI Safety," arXiv preprint, July 25, 2016.

Anderson, Hyrum S., and Phil Roth, "EMBER: An Open Dataset for Training Static PE Malware Machine Learning Models," arXiv preprint, April 16, 2018.

Bissell, Kelly, Jacky Fox, Ryan M. LaSalle, and Paolo Dal Cin, *State of Cybersecurity Resilience 2021: How Aligning Security and the Business Creates Cyber Resilience*, Accenture, 2021.

Bland, J. Martin, and Douglas G. Altman, "Multiple Significance Tests: The Bonferroni Method," *BMJ*, Vol. 310, January 21, 1995.

Branwen, Gwern, "The Neural Net Tank Urban Legend," *Gwern.net* blog, July 4, 2023.

Canadian Institute for Cybersecurity, "CSE-CIC-IDS2018 on AWS," University of New Brunswick, webpage, undated. As of September 1, 2022:
https://www.unb.ca/cic/datasets/ids-2018.html

Chen, Tianqi, and Carlos Guestrin, "XGBoost: A Scalable Tree Boosting System," *Proceedings of the 22nd ACM Special Interest Group on Knowledge Discovery and Data Mining (SIGKDD) International Conference on Knowledge Discovery and Data Mining*, San Francisco, California, August 13–17, 2016.

Computer Security Resource Center, Glossary, "intrusion," webpage, National Institute of Standards and Technology, undated. As of August 4, 2022:
https://csrc.nist.gov/glossary/term/intrusion

Geist, Edward, Aaron B. Frank, and Lance Menthe, *Understanding the Limits of Artificial Intelligence for Warfighters: Vol. 4, Wargames*, RR-A1722-4, 2024.

Gholamy, Afshin, Vladik Kreinovich, and Olga Kosheleva, "Why 70/30 or 80/20 Relation Between Training and Testing Sets: A Pedagogical Explanation," Departmental Technical Reports (Computer Science), University of Texas at El Paso, February 2018.

Gröger, Christoph, "There Is No AI Without Data," *Communications of the ACM*, Vol. 64, No. 11, November 2021.

Harang, Richard, and Ethan M. Rudd, "SOREL-20M: A Large Scale Benchmark Dataset for Malicious PE Detection," arXiv preprint, December 15, 2020.

IBM Institute for Business Value, *AI and Automation for Cybersecurity: How Leaders Succeed by Uniting Technology and Talent*, IBM, June 2022.

IBM Security, *X-Force Threat Intelligence Index 2022*, IBM, February 2022.

Justel, Ana, Daniel Peña, and Rubén Zamar, "A Multivariate Kolmogorov-Smirnov Test of Goodness of Fit," *Statistics & Probability Letters*, Vol. 35, No. 3, October 1997.

Ke, Guolin, Qi Meng, Thomas Finley, Taifeng Wang, Wei Chen, Weidong Ma, Qiwei Ye, and Tie-Yan Liu, "LightGBM: A Highly Efficient Gradient Boosting Decision Tree," *NIPS'17: Proceedings of 31st Conference on Neural Information Processing Systems*, Curran Associates, December 2017.

Khraisat, Ansam, Iqbal Gondal, Peter Vamplew, and Joarder Kamruzzaman, "Survey of Intrusion Detection Systems: Techniques, Datasets and Challenges," *Cybersecurity*, Vol. 2, No. 20, 2019.

Kulinski, Sean, Saurabh Bagchi, and David I. Inouye, "Feature Shift Detection: Localizing Which Features Have Shifted via Conditional Distribution Tests," *NeurIPS 2020: Thirty-Fourth Conference on Neural Information Processing Systems*, online conference, December 6–12, 2020.

LeCun, Yann, Corinna Cortes, and Christopher J. C. Burges, "The MNIST Database of Handwritten Digits," undated. As of August 30, 2022:
http://yann.lecun.com/exdb/mnist/

LeCun, Yann, Léon Bottou, Yoshua Bengio, and Patrick Haffner, "Gradient-Based Learning Applied to Document Recognition," *Proceedings of the IEEE*, Vol. 86, No. 11, November 1998.

Lohn, Andrew J., Jair Aguirre, Mark Ashby, Benjamin Boudreaux, Jonathan Fujiwara, Gavin S. Hartnett, Daniel Ish, John Speed Meyers, Caolionn O'Connell, and Li Ang Zhang, *Attacking Machine Learning in War*, RAND Corporation, RR-4386-AF, 2020, Not available to the general public.

Lu, Jie, Anjin Liu, Fan Dong, Feng Gu, João Gama, and Guangquan Zhang, "Learning Under Concept Drift: A Review," *IEEE Transactions on Knowledge and Data Engineering*, Vol. 31, No. 12, December 2019.

Menthe, Lance, Li Ang Zhang, Edward Geist, Joshua Steier, Aaron B. Frank, Eric Van Hegewald, Gary J. Briggs, Keller Scholl, Yusuf Ashpari, and Anthony Jacques, *Understanding the Limits of Artificial Intelligence for Warfighters: Vol. 1, Summary*, RR-A1722-1, 2024.

Menthe, Lance, Li Ang Zhang, Gavin Hartnett, Sale Lilly, Kristin von Abel, Benjamin Boudreaux, Nihar Chhatiawala, Gary Briggs, Garrett Close, Jonathan Roberts, and Jared Mondschein, *AI at the Edge: Fielding an Expeditionary AI Capability for Army Intelligence*, RAND Corporation, RR-A1641-1, 2023, Not available to the general public.

Minsky, Marvin, ed., *Semantic Information Processing*, MIT Press, 1968.

Panigrahi, Ranjit, and Samarjeet Borah, "A Detailed Analysis of CICIDS2017 Dataset for Designing Intrusion Detection Systems," *International Journal of Engineering & Technology*, Vol. 7, No. 3, January 2018.

Sanger, David E., and Nicole Perlroth, "Pipeline Attack Yields Urgent Lessons About U.S. Cybersecurity," *New York Times*, May 14, 2021.

Scholl, Keller, Gary J. Briggs, Li Ang Zhang, and John L. Salmon, *Understanding the Limits of Artificial Intelligence for Warfighters: Vol. 5, Mission Planning*, RAND Corporation, RR-A1722-5, 2024.

Sharafaldin, Iman, Arash Habibi Lashkari, and Ali A. Ghorbani, "Toward Generating a New Intrusion Detection Dataset and Intrusion Traffic Characterization," *Proceedings of the 4th International Conference on Information Systems Security and Privacy*, Funchal–Madeira, Portugal, January 22–24, 2018.

U.S. Department of Defense, *Summary: 2018 Department of Defense Cyber Strategy*, 2018.

Verizon, *2022 Data Breach Investigations Report*, 2022.

Wirkuttis, Nadine, and Hadas Klein, "Artificial Intelligence in Cybersecurity," *Cyber, Intelligence, and Security*, Vol. 1, No. 1, January 2017.

Yang, Limin, Arridhana Ciptadi, Ihar Laziuk, Ali Ahmadzadeh, and Gang Wang, "BODMAS: An Open Dataset for Learning Based Temporal Analysis of PE Malware," *2021 IEEE Symposium on Security and Privacy Workshops*, San Francisco, California, May 27, 2021.

Zeadally, Sherali, Erwin Adi, Zubair Baig, and Imran A. Khan, "Harnessing Artificial Intelligence Capabilities to Improve Cybersecurity," *IEEE Access*, Vol. 8, 2020.

Zetter, Kim, "Hacker Lexicon: What Is Zero Day?" *Wired Magazine*, November 11, 2014.

Zhang, Li Ang, Yusuf Ashpari, and Anthony Jacques, *Understanding the Limits of Artificial Intelligence for Warfighters: Vol. 3, Predictive Maintenance*, RAND Corporation, RR-A1722-3, 2024.